AF249114

NAME: *BIG JOHN STUDD*

BIRTHDAY: *February 19*

HOMETOWN: *Los Angeles, California*

HEIGHT: *6' 10"*　　　**WEIGHT:** *365 lbs.*

FAVORITE ENTERTAINER: *Sylvester Stallone*

LEAST FAVORITE PERSON: *Andre the Giant*

MOST FAMOUS WRESTLING HOLD: *Body Slam*

MOST UNUSUAL CHARACTERISTIC: *Claims no one can slam him.*

HULKSTER'S RATING: *He's mean, tough and good. I know it'll be a hard match whenever I wrestle him.*

Hulk Hogan's™

Guide to WWF® Wrestling Superstars

How the Hulkster Rates the Good and Bad Guys

Photographs by Steve Taylor and Tom Buchanan, Titan Sports, Inc.
Copyright © 1986 Titan Sports, Inc.

Made in the United States of America
ISBN 0-89954-596-3

Antioch Publishing Company
Yellow Springs, Ohio 45387

NAME: *ANDRE THE GIANT*

BIRTHDAY: *May 19*

HOMETOWN: *Grenoble, France*

HEIGHT: *7′ 5″*   **WEIGHT:** *487 lbs.*

FAVORITE ENTERTAINER: *Bamm-Bamm*

LEAST FAVORITE PERSON: *King Kong Bundy*

MOST FAMOUS WRESTLING HOLD: *The Squash*

MOST UNUSUAL CHARACTERISTIC: *Largest professional athlete—8th wonder of the world.*

HULKSTER'S RATING: *Andre is not only big, but strong and clever, too. He may be the best wrestler of all time.*

NAME: *JAKE "THE SNAKE" ROBERTS*

BIRTHDAY: *May 30*

HOMETOWN: *Stone Mountain, Georgia*

HEIGHT: *6' 4"*   **WEIGHT:** *248 lbs.*

FAVORITE ENTERTAINER: *Rashni The Snake Charmer*

LEAST FAVORITE PERSON: *Ricky "The Dragon" Steamboat*

MOST FAMOUS WRESTLING HOLD: *DDT*

MOST UNUSUAL CHARACTERISTIC: *Collection of snakes. Most notable is a 10-foot python named Damion. Carries snake into ring and puts on his fallen opponents.*

HULKSTER'S RATING: *Watch out for Jake and his snake. Let up for a minute and you'll have that snake crawling on you after being knocked out by the DDT.*

NAME: *KING KONG BUNDY*

BIRTHDAY: *November 7*

HOMETOWN: *Atlantic City, New Jersey*

HEIGHT: *6' 5"*　　　**WEIGHT:** *458 lbs.*

FAVORITE ENTERTAINER: *Sylvester The Cat*

LEAST FAVORITE PERSON: *Hulk Hogan*

MOST FAMOUS WRESTLING HOLD: *The "Avalanche"*

MOST UNUSUAL CHARACTERISTIC: *Agility and speed for his size.*

HULKSTER'S RATING: *I don't like Bundy at all. He plays dirty. He's one of the only WWF Wrestlers ever to badly hurt me…and, he had to cheat to do it.*

NAME: *PAUL "MR. WONDERFUL" ORNDORFF*

BIRTHDAY: *October 29*

HOMETOWN: *Tampa, Florida*

HEIGHT: *6' 1"*   **WEIGHT:** *252 lbs.*

FAVORITE ENTERTAINER: *Benedict Arnold*

LEAST FAVORITE PERSON: *Me*

MOST FAMOUS WRESTLING HOLD: *The Pile Driver*

MOST UNUSUAL CHARACTERISTIC: *Just being Mr. Wonderful.*

HULKSTER'S RATING: *No one is better built but you never can really trust that Mr. Wonderful.*

NAME: *JUNK YARD DOG*

BIRTHDAY: *December 13*

HOMETOWN: *Charlotte, North Carolina*

HEIGHT: *6′ 3″* **WEIGHT:** *280 lbs.*

FAVORITE ENTERTAINER: *Vicki Sue Robinson*

LEAST FAVORITE PERSON: *Jimmy Hart*

MOST FAMOUS WRESTLING HOLD: *Head Butt*

MOST UNUSUAL CHARACTERISTIC: *15-foot chain around his neck.*

HULKSTER'S RATING: *JYD is one of the best. He's strong, he's creative and he loves to grab at his opponents.*

NAME: *TITO SANTANA*

BIRTHDAY: *May 10*

HOMETOWN: *Tocula, Mexico*

HEIGHT: *6' 2"*   **WEIGHT:** *244 lbs.*

FAVORITE ENTERTAINER: *El Cordobez*

LEAST FAVORITE PERSON: *Randy ''Macho Man'' Savage*

MOST FAMOUS WRESTLING HOLD: *Figure Four Leg Lock*

MOST UNUSUAL CHARACTERISTIC: *His Latin fire (patience, time, effort).*

HULKSTER'S RATING: *Tito will be the Intercontinental Champ again someday, I'm sure. He's a great athlete.*

NAME: *RANDY "MACHO MAN" SAVAGE*

BIRTHDAY: *November 15*

HOMETOWN: *Sarasota, Florida*

HEIGHT: *6' 3"* **WEIGHT:** *238 lbs.*

FAVORITE ENTERTAINER: *Himself*

LEAST FAVORITE PERSON: *George "The Animal" Steele*™

MOST FAMOUS WRESTLING HOLD: *Flying Elbow Off Top Rope*

MOST UNUSUAL CHARACTERISTIC: *Woman manager, "Miss Elizabeth"*™

HULKSTER'S RATING: *What's a beautiful woman like Miss Elizabeth doing with a guy like Macho Man? He isn't half as great as he thinks he is.*

MACHO
MAN

NAME: *RICKY "THE DRAGON" STEAMBOAT*

BIRTHDAY: *February 28*

HOMETOWN: *Honolulu, Hawaii*

HEIGHT: *6' 0"*   **WEIGHT:** *238 lbs.*

FAVORITE ENTERTAINER: Bruce Lee

LEAST FAVORITE PERSON: Jake "The Snake" Roberts

MOST FAMOUS WRESTLING HOLD: *Body Press Off Top Rope*

MOST UNUSUAL CHARACTERISTIC: Blend of wrestling and martial arts skills.

HULKSTER'S RATING: *With his martial arts skills, "The Dragon" is moving to the top of the WWF. He could be the champ someday.*

NAME: *DAVEY BOY SMITH*

BIRTHDAY: *December 5*

HOMETOWN: *Leeds, England*

HEIGHT: *6' 1"*   **WEIGHT:** *244 lbs.*

FAVORITE ENTERTAINER: *Ozzy Osbourne*

LEAST FAVORITE PERSON: *The Dream Team (Greg "The Hammer" Valentine/Brutus Beefcake)*

MOST FAMOUS WRESTLING HOLD: *Flying Drop Kick*

MOST UNUSUAL CHARACTERISTIC: *One of the most gymnastic athletes in the World Wrestling Federation.*

HULKSTER'S RATING: *What an athlete! He is fast, strong and a true champion.*

NAME: *DYNAMITE KID*

BIRTHDAY: *November 27*

HOMETOWN: *Manchester, England*

HEIGHT: *6' 0"*   **WEIGHT:** *234 lbs.*

FAVORITE ENTERTAINER: *Bryan Adams*

LEAST FAVORITE PERSON: *The Dream Team (Greg "The Hammer" Valentine/Brutus Beefcake)*

MOST FAMOUS WRESTLING HOLD: *Flying Head Butt*

MOST UNUSUAL CHARACTERISTIC: *One of the most gymnastic athletes in the World Wrestling Federation.*

HULKSTER'S RATING: *Like Davey Boy, he is smaller than many WWF stars, but makes up for it with strength, speed and agility.*

The End